# The Complete

# TAO TE CHING

# In Plain English

## STEPHEN LAU

ISBN-13: 978-1532717840
ISBN-10: 1532717849

# DEDICATION

This book is dedicated to all who wish to be wise
and live a life with profound human wisdom.

# CONTENTS

# ONE

## INTRODUCTION TO THE TAO

### What Is the TAO Wisdom?

The TAO (道), also known as The Way or the TAO wisdom, is the ancient wisdom from China more than two thousand years ago. It originated from the ancient classic **Tao Te Ching**, the only book written by **Lao Tzu**, the Chinese sage, who was born with white hair—often considered a sign of old age and wisdom.

*Tao Te Ching* (道德經) is an ancient Chinese classic on human wisdom. This unique piece of literature is one of the most translated books in human history and world literature. The book is a beautiful collection of Chinese wisdom poetry, in which the author expresses his wisdom in living life in all of its beauty and joy, as well as in all of its pain and sorrow. The language is simple and poetic, but controversial and paradoxical.

"My words are easy to understand
and easy to perform,
Yet no man under heaven

knows them or practices them."
(*Tao Te Ching*, Chapter 70)

Above all, the TAO wisdom is inspiring and intriguing.

There are altogether 81 short chapters, expressed in only 5,000 words. It must be pointed out that there was no punctuation in the original text. Given that each word In the Chinese language may be capable of having multiple meanings, the text without any punctuation is open to many different interpretations. A plausible explanation was that Lao Tzu was very much reluctant to express his wisdom in words. As a matter of fact, according to legend, at that time he was at the point of leaving China for Tibet when he was stopped at the city gate and was told by the guard that he had to put down his wisdom in words before he could leave the country. Deliberately and defiantly, he put down his wisdom concisely and precisely in only 5,000 words with no punctuation at all.

The TAO wisdom is intriguing because it is simple and open to various different interpretations. It is like the three blind men, touching different parts of the same elephant, while describing what an elephant may look like.

To illustrate, the following is taken from the first chapter of *Tao Te Ching* with only 59 Chinese characters:

道可道，非常道。名可名，非常名。
無名天地之始；有名萬物之母。

故 常 無 ， 欲 以 觀 其 妙 ; 常 有 ， 欲 以 觀 其
徼 。
此 兩 者 ， 同 出 而 異 名 ， 同 謂 之 玄 。
玄 之 又 玄 ， 眾 妙 之 門 。
(the original Chinese text; the punctuation marks
were subsequently added by scholars)

"The name that can be named is not the eternal
name.
As nameless, it is the origin of all things;
As named, it is the mother of 10,000 things
Ever desireless, one can see the mystery of all
things.
Ever desiring, one sees only their manifestations.
And the mystery itself is the doorway to all
understanding."
(Lao Tzu, *Tao Te Ching*, Chapter 1)

The above is a very close, almost word-for-word,
translation of the original Chinese text.
The following is my own translation in plain
English, as well as my own interpretation, of the first
chapter of *Tao Te Ching* (my own interpretation is
given in brackets):

"If we could understand the Creator or explain
His ways, then He is no longer infinite and
eternal. (Human wisdom is limited and therefore
we can never completely or fully understand the
ways of Nature or the Creator.)
Mankind, once given a name with an identity, Is
only the source, but not the creator, of all things.

(Man invents but does not create something out of nothing; only the Creator, who is nameless with no identity, creates everything out of nothing.)
Ever humble, we see the mystery of all things in the Creator's realm of creation. (With humility, we may understand *why* certain things were created.)
Ever boastful, we see only the manifestations of all things created. (With pride, we see the wonders of our own inventions, but not the mysteries of the Creator's creations.)
And the mystery itself is the pathway to attaining greater spirituality and further understanding of the Creator. (Not knowing everything may lead to further understanding of the purpose of creation by the Creator.)"

The TAO wisdom is profound human wisdom that requires self-intuition to have greater understanding of the Creator, who is in control of anything and everything created by Him; this further understanding may be instrumental in enhancing human wisdom. For this reason, paradoxically, the TAO was later on evolved into a religion (known as Taoism) in China. However, it must be pointed out that the TAO was never intended to be a religion or some religious belief by Lao Tzu; it was meant to show only what *true* human wisdom really is.

# TWO

## ESSENTIALS OF TAO TE CHING

### The TAO Wisdom Essentials

#### *An empty mind*

The TAO wisdom begins with having an empty mind.

What is an empty mind?

An empty mind is more than just "thinking out of the box": it is *reverse* thinking, which is thinking *backward* in order to find out *why* the mind has its current way of thinking in the first place. An empty mindset originated from Lao Tzu:

> "An empty mind with no craving and no expectation helps us letting go.
> Being in the world and not of the world, we attain heavenly grace.
> With heavenly grace, we become pure and selfless.
> And everything settles into its own perfect place."
> (Lao Tzu, **Tao Te Ching**, Chapter 3)

There was the story of a professor visiting a Zen master to find out more about Zen, which is an Eastern philosophy. In the beginning of the visit, the professor kept on talking while the Zen master served him tea. At some point, the Zen master kept pouring tea into the teacup held by the professor even though it was brimming over. The moral of the story is that one must have an empty mind before one can accept new and unconventional ideas. Likewise, to intuit true human wisdom, one must have an empty mind capable of reverse thinking.

An empty mindset frees us from the many shackles of life that may have enslaved and kept us in bondage without our knowing it.

Are you the master or just a slave of your own life?

Oftentimes, we think we are masters of our lives, but in fact we are no more than just slaves. You are the master only when you have complete control over your own life, especially *how* you think and perceive the realities around you.

How do you gain control over your life in terms of dealing with your career, human relationships, time management, and daily stress, among others?

It is not easy because most of us have a *pre-conditioned* mindset that we must do this and do that in order to succeed in all our endeavors in life.

To illustrate, in our subconscious minds, we want to do well, and, to do well, we must set goals; to reach our goals, we must exert efforts; after accomplishing one goal, we need to set another higher goal, and yet another one higher than the previous ones. In the end, our lives may get more complicated and even out of control; as a result, we are no longer masters but only slaves to what we have accomplished for ourselves.

As a further illustration, **Lance Armstrong**, the once-famous-and-now-disgraced cyclist, used performance-enhancing drugs to win his races after his initial success, and that ultimately brought about his downfall and disgrace. He was stripped off all his previously won medals.

The bottom line: Don't let your life careen out of control, and don't live a life with a life of its own! Get your own life back in order!

Life is complex, and contemporary living is very complicated with its many emotional and material clutters and attachments. To live well, we must learn to let go of anything and everything, because they are impermanent and do not last. The desire for simplicity may accelerate the process of letting go as life progresses. An empty mind with reverse thinking may be instrumental in letting go of all attachments in life.

How do we have an empty mind?

Simplicity is the first step toward detachment, which is the key to unlocking the door to happiness. Live a simple lifestyle, deleting all the trimmings of life and living.

"Simplicity is clarity.
It is a blessing to learn from those
with humble simplicity.

Those with an empty mind
will learn to find the Way.

The Way reveals the secrets of the universe:
the mysteries of the realm of creation;
the manifestations of all things created.
The essence of the Way is to show us
how to live in fullness and return to our origin."
(Lao Tzu, **Tao Te Ching**, Chapter 65)

To do just that, you need an empty mind: letting go of anything and everything that you may erroneously believe are important to you. To create an empty mind, you need *mindfulness*, which is acute mental awareness of self and others, as well as of your needs and not just your wants.

## *Mindfulness*

Mindfulness is mental sharpness to know what is happening in the mind that brings about clarity of thinking, which is essential to human wisdom.

There is a close connection between the body and the mind. This body-mind connection in humans affects both the physical and the mental health of an individual, especially how that individual thinks, as well as acts and reacts. It is important to put the mind where the body is. For example, your body is *now* here—reading this book. But your mind may be somewhere else: your mind may be preoccupied with thoughts of the past, the present, or even the future. In other words, your mind may be rambling and disconnected, although you may not be aware of it. A chaotic mind produces adverse and detrimental biological and chemical changes, such as the production of stress hormones, and the reduction of human growth hormone (HGH), among others, that may accelerate the aging process in both the body and the mind.

Mindfulness begins with the body. Becoming mindful of your body in the present moment is putting your mind where your body is. This produces deep relaxation of both the body and mind—an essential element for clarity of thinking that may be the pathway to attaining true human wisdom.

"watchful, like a man crossing a winter stream;
alert, like a man aware of danger;
courteous, like a visiting guest;
yielding, like ice about to melt;
simple, like a piece of uncarved wood;
hollow, like a cave;
opaque, like muddy water."
(Lao Tzu, *Tao Te Ching*, Chapter 15)

"To end our suffering,
find our true nature.

Stilling our thoughts,
our needs become few.
Following our thoughts,
our distractions become more,
and thus living in chaos.

Enlightenment is our true nature.
Meditation helps us find the origin,
and thus ending our suffering."

(Lao Tzu, *Tao Te Ching*, Chapter 52)

## Living in the present

According to Lao Tzu, only the present is real: the past was gone, and the future, which is uncertain and unpredictable, is yet to come. When the mind stays in the present moment, it does not see the ego-self because it does not exist in the present, and only in the self-deceptive and self-delusional human mind, looking back into the past and anticipating the future with expectations to be fulfilled.

In the present moment, with clarity of mind, we see the ultimate truths of self and others, as well as of everything around us. More importantly, we see our past follies in identifying ourselves with our thoughts that have created our ego; we see our present efforts in striving to protect the ego created by ourselves in the past; and we also see our future futilities in expecting that our desires to sustain the ego will be fulfilled.

Living in the present is an awakening to the realities of all things. It affords us an opportunity to look more *objectively* at any given situation, allowing our minds to think more clearly, to separate the truths from the half-truths or the self-deceptions that may have been created in our subconscious minds all along.

"Living in the present moment,
we find natural contentment.
We do not seek a faster lifestyle,

or a better place to be.
We need the essentials of life,
not its extra trimmings.

Living in the present moment,
we focus on the experience of the moment.
Thus, we enjoy every aspect of simple living,
and find contentment in everyone and
everything.

Living in contentment,
we grow old and die,
feeling contented."
(Lao Tzu, *Tao Te Ching*, Chapter 80)

"Therefore, we focus on the present moment,
doing what needs to be done,
without straining and stressing.

To end our suffering,
we focus on the present moment,
instead of our expected result.
So, we follow the natural laws of things."
(Lao Tzu, *Tao Te Ching*, Chapter 63)

## The natural cycle

The truth of the matter is that everything in life must follow the natural cycle, whether we like it or not, and that we must be patient because nothing is within our control, especially our destinies.

"That which shrinks

Must first expand.
That which fails,
Must first be strong.
That which is cast down
Must first be raised.
Before receiving, there must be giving.
This is called perception of the nature of things.
Soft and weak overcome hard and strong."
(Lao Tzu, *Tao Te Ching*, Chapter 36)

*Spontaneity* is the essence of the natural cycle. What goes up must eventually come down; life begets death; day is followed by night—just like the cycle of the four seasons.

"Allowing things to come and go,
following their natural laws,
we gain everything.
Straining and striving,
we lose everything."
(Lao Tzu, *Tao Te Ching*, Chapter 48)

Intuition of spontaneity is an understanding of the *impermanence* of all things: nothing lasts no matter how we strive to keep the impermanent permanent, and everything remains only with that present moment.

"Strong winds come and go.
So do torrential rains.
Even heaven and earth cannot make them last forever."
(Lao Tzu, *Tao Te Ching*, Chapter 23)

## *No judgment and no separation*

According to Lao Tzu, one should not judge others, nor should one separate oneself from others. Being non-judgmental holds the key to attaining balance and harmony in a world of chaos and disharmony. We are not different from others in that we are *all* imperfect, and that is why we should not judge.

## *No choosing and no picking*

Following the natural cycle of all things, we do not need to pick and choose. Picking and choosing is only sickness of the mind: the futility in striving to control what is essentially uncontrollable.

"People naturally avoid loss and seek gain.
But with all things along the Way,
there is no need to pick and choose.
There is no gain without loss.
There is no abundance without lack.
We do not know how and when
one gives way to the other.

So, we just remain in the center of things,
trusting the Creator, instead of ourselves.
This is the essence of The Way."
(Lao Tzu, *Tao Te Ching*, Chapter42)

Picking and choosing is synonymous with control of self, of others, and of everything around, which is against the laws of nature.

"Controlling external events is futility.
Control is but an illusion.
Whenever we try to control,
we separate ourselves from our true nature.
Man proposes; the Creator disposes.
Life is sacred: it flows exactly as it should.
Trusting in the Creator, we return to our breathing,
natural and spontaneous, without conscious control.

In the same manner:
sometimes we have more,
sometimes we have less;
sometimes we exert ourselves,
sometimes we pull back;
sometimes we succeed,
sometimes we fail.

Trusting in the Creator, we see the comings and goings of things,
but without straining and striving to control them."
(Lao Tzu, *Tao Te Ching*, Chapter 29

The TAO wisdom is to embrace *all*, instead of choosing this and picking that. The more we pick and choose, the more stress we create for ourselves, because we often pick and choose the wrong instead of the right.

"Good fortune and misfortune are all in one.

Seeking one and rejecting the other,
we become completely confused.
Striving for goodness and righteousness,
we become evil and wicked."
(Lao Tzu, *Tao Te Ching*, Chapter 58)

The TAO wisdom, however, does not imply that there is no free will or freedom of choice.

"Fame or self, which is dearer?
Self or wealth, which is greater?
Gain or loss, which is more painful?

Accumulating or letting go, which causes more suffering?
Looking for status and security, we find only suffering.
Knowing our true nature, we find joy and peace.
With nothing lacking, the whole world belongs to us."
(Lao Tzu, *Tao Te Ching*, Chapter 44)

Embracing everything is beneficial because it holds the key to *enlightenment*, which is the understanding of what the TAO wisdom is all about.

"The Way to the Creator has no blueprint.
With faith and humility, we seek neither pride nor blame.
Our actions then become righteous and impeccable.
Our lives are illumined with the Creator's light.

Everything that happens to us is beneficial.
Everything that we experience is instructional.
Everyone that we meet, good or bad, becomes
our teacher or student.

We learn from both the good and the bad.
So, stop picking and choosing.
Everything is a manifestation of the mysteries of
creation."
(Lao Tzu, *Tao Te Ching*, Chapter 27)

## *No expectation and no over-doing*

The TAO wisdom emphasizes "wu-wei" (無為):
"Wu" (無) means "no" and "wei" (為) means "doing."
Due to the literal translation of the original text, "wu-
wei" is sometimes misinterpreted as "non-doing,"
and therefore even regarded as a "passive" way of
looking at life by Lao Tzu. "No over-doing" is a more
appropriate translation of "wu-wei."

Contrary to conventional wisdom, which focuses
much on effort, the TAO wisdom emphasizes
"effortless" effort.

"The softest thing in the world
overcomes what seems to be the hardest.

That which has no form
penetrates what seems to be impenetrable.

That is why we exert effortless effort.
We act without over-doing.
We teach without arguing.

This is the Way to true wisdom.
This is not a popular way
because people prefer over-doing."
(Lao Tzu, *Tao Te Ching*, Chapter 43)

"We act without over-action.
We manage without interference.
We enjoy without attachment.

Effrontery is just
an opportunity for loving-kindness.
Great accomplishments are only
a combination of small steps.
Difficult tasks are no more than
a series of easy steps."
(Lao Tzu, *Tao Te Ching*, Chapter 63)

## *Humility and the Ego*

If the TAO wisdom could be summarized in one word, it is the word "humility."
What is humility?
Humility is the enemy of the ego, while pride is its best friend. With humility, we see who we really are, and not who we think or wish we were. With humility, we become aligned with the Creator, who provides us the wisdom in living in this material world. With humility, we do what is necessary, without any over-doing. With humility, we do not pick and choose because we have no expectation of any outcome. With humility, we trust the Creator and believe in the spontaneity of all things created

by Him. With humility, we live in the present, in perfect harmony with self and with others around us.

Without humility, we see ourselves different or separate from others. This *disconnectedness* is not only a source of conflict and disharmony, but also the origin of the ego flaws. With an inflated ego, we see that we are not only different from but often better than others. With an inflated ego, we focus on our cars, our careers, our social circles that distinguish us from our neighbors and others around us. With an inflated ego, we pick and choose—picking and choosing what we think may sustain our ego. With an inflated ego, we do more—and much more—to guarantee all attachments that define our ego.

# THREE

## THE COMPLETE TAO TE CHING

The original text of *Tao Te Ching* contains only 5,000 words without any punctuation mark. There are altogether 82 short but beautiful poems on human wisdom, and the words, carefully selected by Lao Tzu; the chapters or poems do not follow any specific order.

*Tao Te Ching* is one of the most translated books in world literature. My translation of the book is entirely based on my own interpretation of the wisdom of Lao Tzu, and I have expressed it in plain English.

### Chapter 1: The Creator

If His ways could be explained or understood,
the Creator would no longer be infinite.
If He had a name or an identity,
the Creator would no longer be eternal.

Being infinite and eternal,
the Creator is the origin of all things.
Once given a name and an identity,

mankind is only the source of all things.

Ever humble, we see the mysteries of all things created.
Ever proud, we see only the manifestations of all things created.

Only the mysteries, and not the manifestations, show us The Way to true wisdom.

## Chapter 2: Dualistic Existence

With the fall of man, good cannot exist without evil.
Man is born with virtues, but grows up with vices.

Likewise, life and death complement each other.
Heaven is eternal life; hell is everlasting death.
Human existence is therefore dualistic:
it can make heaven out of hell, or hell out of heaven.

Faith and lack of faith go along with each other.
The first will be the last, and the last will be the first.

## Chapter 3: An Empty Mind for Everything

Focusing on status gives us pride, and not humility.
Hoarding worldly riches deprives us of heavenly assets.

An empty mind with no craving and no expectation helps us let go of everything.
Being in the world and not of the world, we attain

heavenly grace.

With heavenly grace, we become pure and selfless.
And everything settles into its own perfect place.

## Chapter 4: Heavenly Grace

Heavenly grace is like a well of water,
free to all, just for the asking.
It is inexhaustible: the bounty of eternal life.
It quenches all human thirst:
the thirst for anger, desires, and vengeance.
Thirsty no more, we find peace and heavenly grace.

It is hidden, but forever present.
It is inconceivable and intangible.
It comes from the Creator, the origin of all things.

## Chapter 5: No Judgment, No Preference

The Creator has no judgment, no preference:
He treats everything and everyone alike.
Every manifestation attests to the mysteries of His
creation.

So, we, too, embrace everything and everyone with
no judgment, no preference.
His grace, never depleting and forever replenishing,
shows us The Way.
Judgment and preference separate us from His
grace, causing attachment.
Only with His grace do we find renewal and rebirth
along The Way.

## Chapter 6: The Identity of the Spirit

The Spirit is as immortal as the Creator.
As the soul of all creations, the Spirit is within the Creator.
As the essence of godliness, the Spirit is like the mother of all.
Its true identity is forever intact and intangible.

It is always present in the hearts of the humble.
It brings perfection because it endures and is eternal.

## Chapter 7: The Watcher and Observer

The Creator seems elusive amid the changes of life.
At times, He seems to have forsaken His creations.
In reality, He is simply observing the comings and goings of their follies.

Likewise, we watch the comings and goings
of our likes and dislikes, of our desires and fears.
But we do not identify with them.
With no judgment and no preference,
we see the mysteries of creation.

## Chapter 8: Be Like Water

The Spirit is just like water flowing to all things.
Its true nature is to give life indiscriminately to all.
It flows to low places, where people reject and despise.

It flows like a river, nurturing everything and everyone on its way.
Its final stop is the ocean, which is its very origin.

Living by the Spirit, we choose a simple and humble lifestyle.
We meditate to enhance our spirituality.
We love our neighbors as ourselves.
We express compassion to all.
We speak with truth and sincerity.
We live in the present moment.
We take action only when necessary.

Without much ado or over-doing, we trust the guidance of the Spirit.
In this manner, life flows like water, fulfilling itself and also everything naturally.

## Chapter 9: Letting Go

Letting go is emptying the mundane,
to be filled with heavenly grace.

Blessed is he who has an empty mind.
He will be filled with knowledge and wisdom from the Creator.
Blessed is he who has no attachment to worldly things.
He will be compensated with heavenly riches.
Blessed is he who has no ego-self.
He will be rewarded with humility to connect with the Creator.
Blessed is he who has no judgment of self and

others.
He will find contentment and empathy in everyone.

Letting go of everything is The Way to the Creator.

## Chapter 10: The Challenge

Can we embrace both good fortunes and
misfortunes in life?
Can we breathe as easily as innocent babies?
Can we see the world created as is without
judgment?
Can we accept both the desirable and the
undesirable?
Can we express compassion to all without being
boastful?
Can we watch the comings and goings of things
without being perturbed?

Saying "yes" to all of the above is spiritual wisdom
from the Creator,
who watches the comings and goings in the world
He created.

## Chapter 11: The Invisible and the Intangible

The spokes and the hub are the visible parts of a
wheel.
Clay is the visible material of a pot, which is useful
because it contains.
Walls, doors, and windows are visible parts of a
house.

We always look for the visible and the tangible without.
But what really matters is the invisible and the intangible within.

## Chapter 12: The Mysteries of What Is Within

The more we look, the less we see.
The more we hear, the less we listen.
The more we crave, the crazier we become.

What is materialistic is separate from what is spiritualistic.
Therefore, value what is within, and not what is without.

## Chapter 13: Success and Failure

Success and failure are no more than expressions of the human condition.
So, accept both gracefully and willingly, with no judgment, no preference.
The Creator loves us unconditionally, irrespective of our success or failure.
What is meant by "accept both gracefully and willingly"?
Success is avoiding failure; avoiding failure is seeking success.
Both originate from fear and pride: the sources of human suffering.

Seeing ourselves indiscriminately as everything, including success and failure, we see not only the manifestations but also the mysteries of the creation.

## Chapter 14: The Unfathomed Truth

Look, it is invisible.
Listen, it is inaudible.
Grab, it is intangible.

These three characteristics are indefinable:
Therefore, they are joined as one, just like the Creator—invisible, inaudible, and intangible.

As one, it is unbroken thread with neither a beginning nor an end.
It returns to nothingness: invisible, inaudible, and intangible.
It is the indefinable, the intangible, and the unimaginable.
Stand before it, and there is no beginning.
Follow it, and there is no end.
Only by its grace can we discover how things have been and will be.
This is the essence of the Creator: invisible, inaudible, and intangible.

## Chapter 15: The Enlightenment

The ancient prophets were wise.
Their wisdom was unfathomable.
It is indispensable to understanding the salvation from the Creator.

All we can do is to live by their profound prophecies:
watchful, like a man crossing a winter stream;
alert, like a man aware of danger;
courteous, like a visiting guest;
yielding, like ice about to melt;
simple, like a piece of uncarved wood;
hollow, like a cave;
opaque, like muddy water.

Living by their prophecies, we wait for our muddled thoughts to settle,
our composed minds to become clear just like muddy water, until enlightenment arises, followed by eternal salvation.

## Chapter 16: Focusing on the Creator

Life lives itself in us, when we focus on the Creator.
From that focal point, around which all of life revolves.

We watch everything come and go,
with no judgment, no preference.
Everything that is, was, or ever will be,
will return to its origin: the Creator.

Understanding the comings and goings of things,
we fret not, and judge not.
Focusing on the Creator,
we are open to all of life.
Opening to all of life,
we embrace all with thankfulness for what we get,
with gratitude for not getting what we deserve.

Discovering the true nature of things,
we live with compassion and loving-kindness.
All endings become beginnings, all returning to the
Creator.

## Chapter 17: No Separate Self

The greatest virtue of all is to be unaware of a
separate self at all.
Awareness of a separate self makes us want to
become valuable.
Not becoming valuable, we tend to hate the
separate self.
Hating the separate self, how can we value anyone
else?

Freedom from the ego-self, we are free to act
without the desire to be valuable.
As a result, everything is done, and people all say:
"It happened *naturally*."

## Chapter 18: The Differences

In the absence of the Creator, we forget who we
really are.
Then we turn to other things to define who we are,
what is good and moral.

In the presence of the Creator, we act according to
our hearts,
instead of relying on rules and regulations from
those above us.

Rules and regulations may bring fairness and justice,
but no more than a pretense of life.
A pretense of life is our inability to love indiscriminately.
Then we insist on those above us to heal our suffering,
which originates from ourselves.

## Chapter 19: Self-Intuition

Stop striving to be righteous and wise to attain salvation,
which comes not from our efforts, not something we must earn.
Stop abiding by rules and regulations to secure fairness and justice.
Compassion and loving-kindness come naturally to us.
Stop accumulating riches by being smart.
Heavenly assets are freely available to all.

The above are merely superficial suggestions.
The ultimate truths have to be self-intuited:
be simple, be selfless, and be non-judgmental.
Enlightenment may arrive effortlessly.

## Chapter 20: The Creator's Wisdom

We are all desirous of making the right choices,
fearful of making the wrong ones.
We all pursue what others say is good,
avoiding what they say is bad.

We all follow the popular wisdom of judgment and preference,
instead of the wisdom of the Creator,
requiring us to be undesirous and unperturbed, just like a newborn.

The wisdom of the Creator may seem unreal, and even foolish,
while the worldly wisdom may seem smart and popular.
The Way to enlightenment and salvation is narrow and restricted,
while the way to human folly is open and wide.

The foolish all have goals.
The wise are humble and stubborn.
They alone trust the Creator,
and not the world He created.

## Chapter 21: The Way

The ancient prophets follow The Way to the Creator,
The Way to re-discover our true nature,
which is being one with the Creator.

Seemingly intangible, and seemingly elusive,
The Way leads to the origin of all things,
both visible and invisible.

Since the beginning of the beginning, this has been The Way
to the life force of all things,

both past and present.

Throughout all ages, its name has been preserved.
He is the Creator of, as well as the Witness to, all existence.
Humans intuit this truth, not only by believing it, but also by living it.

## Chapter 22: Everything Is Perfect

Accepting what is, we find perfection in the Creator, as well as in everything created by Him.

What seemingly distorted is in fact truthful.
What seemingly lacking is in fact abundant.
What seemingly exhausted is in fact refreshing.

Possessing little, we become content.
Having too much, we lose the Creator.
Having no ego, we become humbled, and our actions are enlightened.
Having no desire for perfection, our actions are welcome by all.
Having no expectation of result, our actions are selfless and non-judgmental.
Having no goal, our actions are under-doing and never over-doing.

Accepting what is, and finding it to be perfect is not easy.
But that is The Way to the Creator.

## Chapter 23: Nothing Lasts Forever

The Way is of few words.
Actions speak louder than words.
Strong winds come and go.
So do torrential rains.
Even heaven and earth cannot make them last
forever.

Why then so much concern over what to say, or
what to do?
Living is but an expression of the life given by the
Creator.
Our true nature is a reflection of that expression.
Those who are with the Creator, the Creator is also
with them.
So, success and failure are seen as part of a perfect
whole.
Everything is accepted and fully lived accordingly.

## Chapter 24: Falling Short

Reaching out for it, we fall.
Running to catch it, we stumble.
Pretending to become enlightened, we become
confused.
Trying to do it right, we fail.
Looking for praise, we become disappointed.
Holding onto it, we lose.

Letting go of straining, striving, and strutting,
we find the wisdom in the Creator.

## Chapter 25: The Great Mystery

The Way to the Creator existed
before the universe was created.

Its essence is formless and unchanging.
It is present wherever we turn,
providing compassion to all beings.
It comes from the Creator of the universe,
who has no name.
To identify him, call him the Creator.
He can also be called the Great Mystery,
from whom we come, in whom we live, and to whom
we return.

The Way is great, because it is boundless.
Boundless, it is eternally flowing.
Eternally flowing, it is constantly returning.
The Way is great because it leads to our true origin,
the origin of all things in heaven and on earth.

Man follows the earth.
The earth follows the universe.
The universe follows the Creator.
The Creator follows Himself.
Hence, He is the greatest of all.

## Chapter 26: Be Stable and Unmoved

The Way to the Creator is deep-rooted.
Unmoved, it is the source of all movement.
Stable, it enables us to act without rashness.

So, whatever we do, we do not abandon our true nature.
The world around us is riddled with worries and distractions.
We remain stable, steady, and steadfast.

We do not let ourselves be blown to and fro.
Otherwise, we lose touch with who we really are;
or, worse, who the Creator is.

## Chapter 27: Pick Not, Choose Not

The Way to the Creator has no blueprint.
With faith and humility, we seek neither pride nor blame.
Our actions then become righteous and impeccable.
Our lives are illumined with the Creator's light.

Everything that happens to us is beneficial.
Everything that we experience is instructional.
Everyone that we meet, good or bad, becomes our teacher or student.

We learn from both the good and the bad.
So, stop picking and choosing.
Everything is a manifestation of the mysteries of creation.

## Chapter 28: Trusting the Creator

Striving to climb the ladder of success,
we may seem smart.
But trusting our Creator,

we find divine guidance,
which is effortless along the Way.

Striving to be right or wrong according to the world,
we may seem righteous.
But trusting our Creator,
we find potentials of our true nature,
which express compassion and loving-kindness to
all.

Being charismatic,
we may seem popular.
But trusting our Creator,
we find our true nature.

Separating from our true nature,
we struggle with forms and functions.
Returning to our true nature,
we find ourselves being one with the Creator.

## Chapter 29: Letting Go Control

Controlling external events is futility.
Control is but an illusion.
Whenever we try to control,
we separate ourselves from our true nature.
Man proposes; the Creator disposes.
Life is sacred: it flows exactly as it should.
Trusting in the Creator, we return to our breathing,
natural and spontaneous, without conscious control.

In the same manner:
sometimes we have more,

sometimes we have less;
sometimes we exert ourselves,
sometimes we pull back;
sometimes we succeed,
sometimes we fail.

Trusting in the Creator, we see the comings and goings of things,
but without straining and striving to control them.

## Chapter 30: Simplify the Doing

Letting go control,
we no longer strive and struggle.
Without strife and struggle,
there is no resistance.
Without resistance,
there is no suffering.

Living in the present moment,
we see all things that we must do.
Without complaint and resistance, we do them accordingly.
Without seeking control and recognition,
we simplify what we do, however complicated they may be.
Trusting in the Creator, we always under-do and never over-do.

## Chapter 31: Forgiveness

Vengeance and violence
are not along The Way to the Creator,

no matter how justified they may be.
Faced with vengeance and violence,
remember the Creator's precepts:
forgive our enemies;
love our neighbors as ourselves.

An eye for an eye
makes us become what we hate.
Knowing this, we do not
rejoice in victory over our enemies,
nor take delight in their downfall.

Victory is but an illusion;
getting even gains us nothing.
Once vengeance and violence are over,
there is nothing left but our own pain.

## Chapter 32: Beyond Words

What we call the Creator really has no name.
He is intangible and unfathomable.

We experience Him in our own true nature.
If we are one with Him, peace comes upon our lives,
like soft rain falling from heaven,
like joy rising from the earth,
like a mighty river flowing.
Our world then becomes a paradise,
and natural goodness is written in our hearts.

Since the beginning of the beginning,
there have been names for everything.

The more words we use,
the more distinctions we make.
The more distinctions we have,
the more we pick and choose.
As a result, we separate ourselves
from our own true nature.

To return to peace and harmony,
we must be like rivers and streams,
returning to their origin—the ocean.

## Chapter 33: True Wisdom

Knowing others is intelligence.
Knowing ourselves is true wisdom.
Overcoming others is strength.
Overcoming ourselves is true power.

Understanding that we have everything we need,
we count our blessings.
Identifying with our own true nature,
we hold fast to what endures.

## Chapter 34: Like A Great Ocean

The Creator is like an ocean.
It fills everything and everywhere.
It is the origin of life.
It never abandons its creations.
It accomplishes, but needs no recognition.
It nourishes and cherishes all,
yet gives everyone the freedom to choose.
It has no need for glory,

so it retreats to the background
and becomes inconspicuous.
Yet we all return to it.
And that is why it is great.
Its greatness needs no recognition.

Likewise, our greatness comes
not from our power or control,
but from our own true nature,
which is living as one with the Creator.

## Chapter 35: Spreading the Truth

Living as one with the Creator,
there is no danger, only peace and harmony.
Lively music and gourmet food
may make people stay.
But spreading the truth about the Creator
may be unexciting and unattractive to many.
People prefer misleading distractions.
People love empty promises.

The truth about the Creator
is profound but unpopular.
Look at it; it is invisible.
Listen to it; it is inaudible.
Use it; it is inexhaustible.

## Chapter 36: The Natural Laws

Before we can shrink anything,
we must first let it expand.
Before we can get rid of something,

we must first let it flourish.
Before we can receive something,
we must first give it away.
They are called the natural laws
of the way things were, are, and will be.

The soft overcomes the hard.
The slow overcomes the fast.
Gentleness and flexibility
bring positive results
that force and rigidity
fail to produce.
Just trust the natural laws
of the mighty Creator.

## Chapter 37: Everything in Its Natural Place

The Creator never seems to do anything,
yet all things are done accordingly.

We stay in the very center of the Creator,
and refrain from controlling our destiny.
Everything will evolve and fall into its natural place,
according to the natural laws of the Creator.

When there is no desire to be someone that we are
not,
separate from our true nature designed by the
Creator,
all things are in perfect balance and harmony.

## Chapter 38: The Contrived and the Natural

The Creator has no wish to be powerful;
and thus he is truly powerful.
The ordinary man craves to be powerful;
and thus he never has enough power.

The Creator does nothing,
yet nothing is left undone.
The ordinary man is always doing things,
yet there are always many more to be done.

With the grace of the Creator,
we experience natural goodness.
Natural goodness requires no effort,
no expectation of reward or recognition.
Contrived goodness requires great effort,
with little or no accomplishment.
Compassion and loving-kindness seek nothing.
Fairness and justice demand results,
with expectation of correct behavior.
Natural goodness comes from within,
which is our essence,
and not from without,
which is only our appearance.

When we are separate from our true nature,
we experience no natural goodness,
no compassion and no loving-kindness.
Our goodness then becomes contrived,
demanding fairness and justice,
focusing on appearance and superficiality.

## Chapter 39: Dependent on the Creator

Dependent on the Creator,
our horizons broaden and expand,
our souls inspire and nourish,
our relationships grow and flourish.
Everything around us becomes oneness with the
Creator.

Dependent on ourselves,
our horizons contract and shrink,
our souls wither and die,
our relationships break and crumble.
Everything around us becomes depleted and
damaged.

Do not strive for prestige and power.
They all belong to the Creator.
Only with humility can we connect with Him.
Humility is The Way to Him.
Dependent on the Creator,
we do not strive to be shiny like jade.
but just dull like stones.

## Chapter 40: Being Born of Non-Being

Following The Way,
we return to our root.
On The Way,
yielding is the way to go.

Everything in the universe
depends on everything else.
Even living our life experience
depends on how we think of death.

## Chapter 41: The Enigma

When a wise man hears of the Creator,
he immediately begins to do some soul-searching.
When an average man hears of the Creator,
he half believes Him, and half doubts Him.
When a foolish man hears of the Creator,
he laughs out loud.
If he did not laugh,
there would be no Creator.

Thus it is said:
The Way to the light seems dark.
The Way forward seems to go backward.

The Way direct seems long.
True power seems week.
True purity seems tarnished.
True steadfastness seems changeable.
True clarity seems obscure.
The greatest seems inconspicuous.
The greatest love seems indifferent.
The greatest wisdom seems foolish.

The Creator is hidden and nameless.
Yet He nourishes and completes all things.

## Chapter 42: Remaining in the Center

The Creator creates one.
One creates two.
Two creates three.

Three creates a myriad of things.

All have their original unity
in the duality of *yin* and *yang*,
the opposite life forces that harmonize.
We experience this harmonious process
in the rising and falling of our breaths.

People naturally avoid loss and seek gain.
But with all things along The Way,
there is no need to pick and choose.
There is no gain without loss.
There is no abundance without lack.
We do not know how and when
one gives way to the other.

So, we just remain in the center of things,
trusting the Creator, instead of ourselves.
This is the essence of The Way.

## Chapter 43: Effortless Effort

The softest thing in the world
overcomes what seems to be the hardest.

That which has no form
penetrates what seems to be impenetrable.

That is why we exert effortless effort.
We act without over-doing.
We teach without arguing.

This is The Way to true wisdom.

This is not a popular way
because people prefer over-doing.

## Chapter 44: The Choices

Fame or self, which is dearer?
Self or wealth, which is greater?
Gain or loss, which is more painful?

Accumulating or letting go, which causes more
suffering?
Looking for status and security, we find only
suffering.
Knowing our true nature, we find joy and peace.
With nothing lacking, the whole world belongs to us.

## Chapter 45: Perfectly Done

True perfection seems imperfect,
yet it is perfectly flawless.
True abundance seems lacking,
yet it is fully present.

True honesty seems hypocritical.
True wisdom seems foolish.
True eloquence seems hesitant.

When the Creator is in control,
we act with effortless effort.
What is needed is perfectly done.

## Chapter 46: Lasting Satisfaction

Trusting the Creator, we concentrate on the Creator.
Relying on ourselves, we focus on our ego.

Our greatest suffering comes from
not knowing who we are, or to whom we belong.
Our greatest unhappiness comes from
wanting more than what the Creator provides.
Our greatest satisfaction of contentment
is the lasting satisfaction.

## Chapter 47: Accomplish Without Striving

Without going out the door, we know the world.
Without looking out the window, we see the Creator.
The more we look outside ourselves,
the less we know about anything.

Trusting the Creator, the ancient prophets
knew without doing, understood without seeing.
Trusting the Creator, we accomplish without striving.

## Chapter 48: Need to Do Nothing

Seeking the Creator,
we give up something every day.
The less we have,
the less we need to strain and strive
until we need to do nothing.
Allowing things to come and go,
following their natural laws,
we gain everything.

Straining and striving,
we lose everything.

## Chapter 49: The Creator's Mind

The Creator has no mind of His own.
He works with the mind of everyone.

He is good to those who are good.
He is also good to those who are not so good.
This is godly goodness.

He trusts those who are trustworthy.
He also trusts those who are not so trustworthy.
This is true trust.

The Creator's mind is unfathomable.
People do not understand Him.
They look up to Him and wait.
He treats them like His own children.

## Chapter 50: Life and Death

Life begets death; one is inseparable from the other.
One is form; the other is formless.
Each gives way to the other.

One third of people focus on life, ignoring death.
One third of people focus on death, ignoring life.
One third of people think of neither, just drifting along.
They all suffer in the end.

Trusting the Creator, we have no illusion about life and death.
Holding nothing back from life, we are ready for death,
just as a man ready for sleep after a good day's work.

## Chapter 51: In the Heart of Every Being

Each and every being in the universe
is an expression of the Creator.
We are all shaped and perfected by Him.
Therefore, we should honor the Creator
and delight in His eternal presence,
not because we are commanded,
but because it is our own nature.

The Creator gives birth to all beings,
nourishes and cherishes them,
instructs, comforts, and matures them,
and then returns them to their origin.

The Creator gives us life,
but does not claim to own us.
He is always acting on our behalf,
but expects nothing in return.
He is guiding us along The Way,
but does not control where we turn.
His presence is deep within us,
in the very nature of our being.

## Chapter 52: Finding the Origin

In the beginning was the Creator.
All things originate from Him.
All things return to Him.

To find the origin,
look for His manifestations.
To find the mother,
recognize her children.
To end our suffering,
find our true nature.

Stilling our thoughts,
our needs become few.
Following our thoughts,
our distractions become more,
and thus living in chaos.

Enlightenment is our true nature.
Meditation helps us find the origin,
and thus ending our suffering.

## Chapter 53: Distracting Detours

The Way is easy,
yet people prefer distracting detours.
Beware when things are out of balance.
Remain centered within the Creator.

Distractions are many,
in the form of riches and luxuries.
They allure us from The Way.

Accumulations are like extortions of the poor.

They bring only disaster and suffering.
Do not deviate from The Way.

## Chapter 54: The Presence of the Creator

When we are planted in the Creator,
we will not be easily rooted up.
When we are embraced by the Creator,
we will never slip away.

If the Creator is present in our lives,
our lives will express our true nature.
If the Creator is present in our families,
our families will experience prosperity.

If the Creator is present in our countries,
our countries will set good examples
to all other countries in the world.
If the Creator is present in the universe,
the universe will delight in virtues.

How do we know this is true?
By looking inside ourselves,
when we observe the comings and goings
of everything and everyone around us.

## Chapter 55: In Natural Harmony

If we are in harmony with the Creator,
we are like newborn babies,
in natural harmony with all.
Our bones are soft, and our muscles are weak,
but our grip is strong and powerful.

Not knowing about sex,
we manifest sexual arousal.
Crying all day long,
we lose not our voice.
With constancy and harmony,
we accomplish all daily tasks
without growing tired.

In natural harmony with the Creator,
we let all things come and go,
exerting no effort, showing no desire,
and expecting no result.
Natural harmony is experienced
only in the present moment,
when we see the natural laws of the Creator.

## Chapter 56: No Longer Matters

The more we understand The Way,
the less we need to convince others.
Those, who speak much,
know little about The Way.

So, we no longer argue with those who are cynical.
We stop looking for their approval.
We cease taking offense at their unbelief.
We just sow the seeds along The Way,
letting the Creator reap the harvest.

To be loved or rejected,
to gain or to lose,
to be approved or disapproved,
no longer matters to us,

when we know who we are
and who the Creator is.

## Chapter 57: More for Less

To guide a great country, we need a great ruler.
To wage a successful war, we need good strategies.
To live a life of harmony, we need letting life live by itself.

That essentially means:
the more efforts we exert, the more failures we experience;
the more weapons we make, the more dangers we encounter;
the more laws we enact, the more law-breakers we produce.

So, follow The Way.
Stop striving to change ourselves: we are naturally changing.
Stop striving to be good: we are naturally good.
Stop striving to get rich: we are naturally abundant.
Stop striving to control destiny: life is naturally living itself.

## Chapter 58: The Pure and Simple Way

The Way to the Creator is pure and simple.
If The Way were interfering and complicated,
it would be painful and difficult to follow.

Good fortune and misfortune are all in one.
Seeking one and rejecting the other,
we become completely confused.
Striving for goodness and righteousness,
we become evil and wicked.

To follow The Way,
we need principles,
but without imposing on others;
we need honesty,
but without being unkind to others;
we need consistency,
but without taking advantage of others.
We set an example for others
to follow The Way to the Creator.

## Chapter 59: The Golden Mean

To serve others and the Creator,
there is nothing better than the golden mean.

With the golden mean, there is moderation.
With moderation, our limits are unknown.
With unknown limits, our potentials are infinite.
With infinite potentials, our power is everlasting.
With the golden mean, we accommodate ourselves
to
the ever-changing world around us.
We simplify the complicated with gentle ease,
like a mother caring for her child.

Deep rooted in the presence of the golden mean,
we follow The Way, and never lose our way.

## Chapter 60: Frying a Small Fish

Living our lives is like frying a small fish;
we neither over-season nor over-cook it.

Centering ourselves in the Creator,
we have neither fear nor worry.
It is not that they no longer exist,
but that they no longer have power over us.
So, they diminish and disappear from our lives.

Walking along The Way is like frying a small fish.
We used to suffer; now we have become wise.

## Chapter 61: A Great Nation

A great country is like a sea,
with all streams flowing into it.
The more powerful it is,
the greater its need for humility.
Humility means trusting the Creator
in deference to The Way.

A great nation is like a great man.
When he makes a mistake,
not only does he realize it,
but also admit it.
He learns from his mistakes:
everyone is his teacher,
and his enemy is his own shadow.

If a great nation is centered in the Creator,

it cherishes and nourishes all its citizens;
it is a shining light to all other nations in the world.

## Chapter 62: Abiding in the Creator

The Creator is in the center of the universe,
the refuge of those who abide in Him,
and the protector of those who ignore Him.

Honors can be bought with fine words;
respect can be won with good deeds.
Abiding in the Creator is beyond all values.

Thus, there is no greater gift of wealth and power
than showing The Way to the Creator,
just like the ancient prophets did.

Why did the ancient prophets follow The Way?
Because seeking the Creator,
we shall find what we need;
we shall find forgiveness
for the wrong we have done.
That is why everybody loves it.

## Chapter 63: The Present Moment

We act without over-action.
We manage without interference.
We enjoy without attachment.

Effrontery is just
an opportunity for loving-kindness.
Great accomplishments are only

a combination of small steps.
Difficult tasks are no more than
a series of easy steps.

Therefore, we focus on the present moment,
doing what needs to be done,
without straining and stressing.

To end our suffering,
we focus on the present moment,
instead of our expected result.
So, we follow the natural laws of things.

## Chapter 64: A Small Step

We need a still and composed mind
to see things with greater clarity.
Because trouble begins in the mind
with small and unrelated thoughts.
So, we carefully watch the mind
to stop any trouble before it begins.

Thus we put things in order
before they become out of order.

The great pine tree
springs from a tiny sprout.
The journey of a thousand miles
begins with the first step.

Accordingly, we do not rush into things.
We neither strain nor stress.
We let go of success and failure.

We patiently take the next necessary step,
a small step and one step at a time.
We relinquish our conditioned thinking.
Being our true nature, we help all beings
return to their own true nature too.

## Chapter 65: Humble Simplicity

The ancient prophets used simple ways
to teach The Way to the Creator.

Those, who think they know, know not The Way.
Those, who think they know not, find The Way.

Simplicity is clarity.
It is a blessing to learn from those
with humble simplicity.
Those with an empty mind
will learn to find The Way.
The Way reveals the secrets of the universe:
the mysteries of the realm of creation;
the manifestations of all things created.
The essence of The Way is to show us
how to live in fullness and return to our origin.

## Chapter 66: The Power of Humility

Rivers and streams generate great power
as they flow down to the ocean below.
The power is in the downward movement

Humility is power.
Power comes from the lowly.

According to The Way:
the lowly will be elevated;
the last will be the first.

The Creator is above,
and we are below.

The Creator is in front,
and we are behind.
Because this is the nature of things,
humility is only natural to us.
Yet many are desirous of the top
fearful of lagging behind.
Humility is The Way.

## Chapter 67: The Three Essentials

The Way may seem insignificant.
It is because it appears ordinary.
The Way is great beyond comparison.
If there were any comparison,
it would no longer be great.

The Way is great because of its three essentials:
compassion, humility, and faith.
With compassion, there is no fear.
With humility, there is no strife.
With faith, there is no impossibility.

Without compassion, fearlessness becomes
ruthlessness.
Without humility, efforts become complicated and
difficult.

Without faith, possibilities become controlling and self-centering.

Compassion is the root.
Humility is the stem.
Faith is the flower.

## Chapter 68: Not Seeking Our Way

We do not become aggressive when we are confronted.
We do not become angry when we are provoked.
We see neither an enemy nor a competitor,
because we do not seek our own way.

Knowing both our strengths and weaknesses,
we use them to complement one another.
Thus, we find balance and harmony.
Naturally and easily, we follow The Way.

## Chapter 69: Become Our Own Enemy

According to military strategies,
defense is preferred to attack;
consolidation is better than overextension.

So, we advance
not at the expense of overstepping anyone.

So, we gain
not at the expense of making anyone lose.
So, we accomplish
not at the expense of straining ourselves.

We have no enemy.
We love everyone as ourselves.
We remain in our true nature;
otherwise, we lose
the three essentials of The Way,
and become our own enemy.

## Chapter 70: Easy to Find and Follow

The Way is easy to find and follow:
empty the mind of conditioned thinking
of seeing things and doing things.

The Way comes from the source of all.
Its power cherishes and nourishes all.
Knowing the source, we know ourselves.

Finding The Way,
we know the nature of things;
we see the comings and goings of things.

Following The Way,
we discover the treasures within;
we simplify the trappings without.
So, we continue The Way with inner joy.

## Chapter 71: The Importance of Knowing

Not knowing The Way,
but pretending we know,
we remain ignorant, and suffer.

Knowing that we do not know,
we pursue its wisdom:
knowing its origin,
knowing its ending,
and knowing our true nature.

## Chapter 72: In Awe of the Creator

Without awe of the mysteries of the Creator,
we are easily controlled by fear.
Without self-love and compassion for others,
we are easily victimized by others.

Knowing our true nature,
we know who we are,
and what we need.
We accomplish things
without taking credit or reward.
We cherish ourselves
without separating us from other beings.
We nourish our external identity
without forgetting our inner reality.

## Chapter 73: Nothing Slips Through

We try to be good, and do the best we can,
yet sometimes bad things happen to us.
We have no explanation for that.

We just follow The Way,
one step at a time,
accepting the good and the bad,
as essential parts of life.

We quietly respond to every situation
with neither strain nor stress.

We trust the Creator.
His net, vast and loose,
covers the whole universe,
and nothing slips through.
He controls all.

## Chapter 74: Unnatural Fear of Death

Abiding in the Creator, we do not fear death.
Following the conditioned mind, we fear everything.
Fear is a futile attempt to control things and people.

Death is a natural destination of The Way.
Unnatural fear of death does more harm than good.
It is like trying to use intricate tools of a master craftsman:
we end up hurting ourselves.

## Chapter 75: Never Really Live

When there is abundance, there is lack.
When there is craving, there is discontentment.
Striving for power to control and influence
every aspect of our lives
is the source of our suffering.

Obsessed with getting and keeping,
many of us never really live before we die.

Following The Way,

we must learn to let go.

## Chapter 76: Soft and Yielding

At birth, we are soft and supple.
At death, we are stiff and hard.
Young plants are tender and pliant.
Dead plants are brittle and dry.

Stiff and inflexible, we are like death.
Soft and yielding, we are like life.

Following The Way,
we become soft and supple.
That is why we always prevail,
because tenderness and flexibility
give us strength and power from the Creator.

## Chapter 77: Like Bending a Bow

Following The Way is like bending a bow:
one end is pulled up;
the other end is pulled down.
Excess and deficiency are balanced.

According to wisdom of The Way:
we reduce when there is excess;
we increase when there is deficiency.
Balance is thus created.

According to common wisdom:
we increase excess and deplete deficiency.
Imbalance is thus created.

Following The Way,
we follow our true nature:
giving without worrying;
receiving without attaching.

## Chapter 78: The Paradox

The Way is paradoxical.
Like water, soft and yielding,
yet it overcomes the hard and the rigid.
Stiffness and stubbornness cause much suffering.

We all intuitively know
that flexibility and tenderness
are The Way to go.
Yet our conditioned mind
tells us to go the other way.

We accept all that is simple and humble.
We embrace the good fortune and the misfortune.
Thus, we become masters of every situation.
We overcome the painful and the difficult in our
lives.
That is why The Way seems paradoxical.

## Chapter 79: True Contentment

Resentment breeds more resentment.
Only contentment leads to contentment.
True contentment comes from our true nature:
not from what we do, or how we do;
neither from our status nor our control.

The Creator is impartial.
No one is special.

## Chapter 80: Feeling Contented

Living in the present moment,
we find natural contentment.

We do not seek a faster lifestyle,
or a better place to be.
We need the essentials of life,
not its extra trimmings.

Living in the present moment,
we focus on the experience of the moment.
Thus, we enjoy every aspect of simple living,
and find contentment in everyone and everything.

Living in contentment,
we grow old and die,
feeling contented.

## Chapter 81: True Wisdom

The truth is unpleasant to the ear.
What is pleasant to the ear is not the truth.
Likewise, true wisdom is unpopular;
what is popular is not true wisdom.

The wise learn to let go, instead of accumulating.
The wise learn to succumb, instead of arguing.
The wise find the Way, not from knowledge,

but from their own true nature.

Without straining and striving for control,
we discover what life really is:
following The Way to the Creator.

## THE END

# APPENDIX

## ABOUT STEPHEN LAU

### About Stephen Lau:

http://www.stephencmlau.com

### Stephen Lau's Blog:

http://www.reflectionsofstephenlau.blogspot.com

### Stephen Lau's Related Websites:

http://www.daily-tao-wisdom.com
http://www.wisdominliving.com
http://www.health-and-wisdom-tips.com
http://www.chinesenaturalhealing.com
http://www.wisdom-from-books.com

### Books by Stephen Lau:

http://www.booksbystephenlau.com

### Contact Stephen Lau

stephencmlau@gmail.com

Made in United States
North Haven, CT
10 September 2023

41337527R00046